Inspiring Bold

Laura Kempf

ISBN: 1718779933
ISBN-13:978-1718779938

DEDICATION

Dedicated to the love of my life, Scott, and the best children anyone could ask for, Elise and Lincoln.

CONTENTS

ACKNOWLEDGMENTS

Thank you to all my teachers, from whom I have learned so much. I am listing a few but grateful for you all:

My family for making me who I am today;

Mahesh Visvanathan, for supporting me in all the BOLD things I do (including this book);

Julie Whitworth, for being my devil's advocate;

Business Transformation group in Watson Health for positivity and support;

Prior Sensei and Gemba coaches who put their hearts into what they do;

Watson Health employees engaged on the Lean journey and working hard to change the world;

Mindfulness@IBM for teaching me mindfulness;

Zingerman's Mail Order and Ari Weinzweig, for sharing their Lean journey;

Michigan Yoga Room, for reminding me to do what I can on my own mat;

Michigan Lean Consortium, for giving me a place to grow;

My old finance and accounting department for putting up with me as a manager; and

All my mentors and those who were willing to provide guidance over the years.

PREFACE

Like the title says, I wrote this book to inspire. Inspire what? Change. Improvement. Transformation. Particularly "bold" change because this is the type of impact we always sought in our Lean events. I describe these events in more detail later in the book but at the heart of it, a Lean event brings together empowered employees to make substantial change in the work they do.

"Inspiring Bold" is about change for everyone. For employees. For you. For anyone willing to listen. It costs you nothing other than the minimal price of this book. But for that price, I take you on my journey and let you shadow my experiences, which is the best kind of learning, aside from going through it yourself. It is up to you to take it forward after reading this book. It is up to you to reflect on the stories here and what you can do better. It is up to you to take a hard look at yourself and make a change, and start to see the world in a different light.

Please do so, because it is a gut-wrenching task to write a book like this. It's my heart and soul with imperfections in tow, put on a platter for the world to see. I have learned a whole new sense of appreciation for anyone who publishes, especially for those who self-publish and do not usually recoup profits. But this book has never been about money. It is only about getting the message out there and sharing my journey.

I want to thank those who made it possible. To my loving husband, Scott, and sweet kids, Elise and Lincoln, thank you for putting up with the writing on the nights and weekends. To all my teachers over the years, both in the Lean world and prior. Thank you. Some of you may not have even known it. Some of you may be in this book, but no worries. Just as in the Lean events, Vegas rules apply. What takes place in the event, stays in the event. Only the story is mentioned with my reflection. It doesn't matter who the characters are. Enjoy!

ONCE I WAS BLIND…

Like everything else with Lean, current state (how things were before changing them) seems like the appropriate place to start. In this case, the current state is me. The "me" before I started my Lean journey, in my earlier leadership roles, and in my childhood. Family plays a key role in making you who you are today. So, let me turn the mirror around and give you an idea who that person was.

I am the middle daughter of three girls raised by a hardworking family in northwest Indiana. I know some of you might stop me right there and say, "I understand." Heck, there is a wine named Middle Sister and a national holiday: August 12 is recognized as National Middle Child Day. Why? The syndrome goes something along the lines of the middle child being left out. The oldest child gets attention first and has years without siblings. In my case, my older sister had five dedicated years. Bet she was happy to see me show up. My younger sister showed up less than two years after me. With the youngest being the last baby in the family, parents soak up every memory. Attention galore.

I don't remember feeling left out though. In my case, I think I may have overcompensated to hold my own in the limelight. It has only taken me forty-some years to realize that who I am today stems so much from how I was raised. My father instilled this feeling of competition amongst us girls. It was all in good fun but that feeling was constantly there. Which one of us had the better grades? Which one was making headlines in sports at school? Honor roll or any special achievements? There was a constant barrage of who had what going for them.

It followed into adulthood. I remember when my sister started working as a dentist and showed her first paycheck to my father, who would relentlessly bring up the six-figure salary to me. It didn't matter that I had a great job. It didn't matter that I had been working while my sister was in school. And it didn't matter that I built sizeable savings versus school loans. Even as an adult, competition was there.

I came to realize that it was this competitive upbringing that saved me from the middle child syndrome and likely gave me one of my strongest and weakest qualities: tenacity. Merriam-Webster defines tenacity (state of being tenacious) as persistence or perseverance, although other synonyms define tenacity in a less positive way: stubbornness or doggedness.

To demonstrate, the example I love to give is how I chose my first career. I remember proudly going to my dad to tell him I was attending the engineering program at Purdue University.

"Engineering. It's not the best career choice for women," he said as he shook his head with disapproval. The decision was made right there. No one was going to tell me that I couldn't follow my dream. Not only did I decide to become an engineer but I chose chemical engineering, one of the hardest curriculums offered. It was a major life choice and I made it final based off a five-minute discussion with my father and tenacity in my back pocket. I was young and it would be some time before I would learn to manage this quality correctly. In fact, I still work to manage it today, but then I am jumping ahead, aren't I?

After receiving my chemical engineering degree, it shouldn't be shocking that I then took a nontraditional route for engineering. I wasn't going to sit in an office. My first position was managing 20 operators at a fertilizer plant in Florida. The company had employed engineers to learn operations and become managers. It was a fast track to leadership, or how I defined leadership at the time: by title. But what I liked was the challenge. So, my tenacity and I took this first step into management where my judgment and perception were being constantly tested. I dug in even harder. I rescheduled your shift if you showed up late (no excuses). I made rounds, ensuring all tasks were completed. I did the job, even the hard stuff. I remember having to suit up in full respiratory gear to test oxygen and temperature levels before sending workers into areas like enclosed tanks. I worked the same shifts as employees and my counterparts: midnights as well as days. Rumors flew around the plant that I was gay. I ignored them but today I still think it's funny. I realized that maybe my dad had this right. Not that I shouldn't do engineering because I was a woman, but maybe it wasn't the right path for me. Maybe he was trying to say that I would enjoy doing something else. Maybe it came out wrong? Or maybe I took it wrong? My dad passed away several years ago, so I can't ask him, but I would put my money on the latter.

After a few jobs in engineering, I decided to get an MBA from University of Chicago. I took my management style with me into finance. At Watson Health (previously Truven Health), I worked my way up from financial analyst to director in finance before switching to Lean.

I established a strong reputation for getting things done and taking on new challenges. One of my proudest accomplishments was when my team and I figured out how to use Oracle to support government accounting. At that time, Deltek was the premier system for government accounting. We had an auditor visit who reviewed our system as satisfactory but noted that Oracle had its limitations. It was the auditor's way of hinting, if you are going to be in the government business, you need a government accounting system. At that time, though, we were owned by a private equity firm and funds were limited. I took a huge risk in signing up to ensure Oracle and our processes would address those limitations in the following year. The team implemented significant change in the underlying setup and existing processes. The following year, the auditor passed us with flying colors. She noted during the audit that it was a "remarkable feat" that she thought couldn't be done.

So, what was I thinking back then? As a manager? As a leader? I can only imagine but I am sure the rhetoric in my head went something like this: I am in charge. I make the call. I assign the employees work. I am the boss. I... I... and so on and so on. Remember, I used to run shifts as a female leader, managing 20 male operators in a plant. That takes some major cojones!

But, that original management style was going to change. After years in a successful finance career, Lean came calling. Once again, I went charging in. Tenacity, full steam ahead. We had bought a niche company (called Simpler) that focused on process improvement, and the executive management team chose to employ Lean internally. I was part of the initial efforts representing finance. A new challenge? I was all in. There was something contagious about Lean. Respecting people. Empowering a culture of problem solvers. Focusing on ways to delight the client. Making decisions based on data versus opinion. Experimenting ("try-storming") versus brainstorming. Establishing management's responsibility to remove barriers for the employees. To me, Lean was about culture transformation and at the heart of it, the employees.

In today's world, there is an abundance of tools (huddles, visual management, eight wastes, etc.) and an abundance of systems (Lean, Agile, Six Sigma, and yes, even Design Thinking). Tools and frameworks help, but business transformation as I describe it above revolves so much more around culture and employee engagement. That's what drew me in. Before I knew it, I was leaving finance behind and taking the position of Business Transformation Consultant or Lean Champion. I no longer had direct reports. I no longer had a management title.

It helps to define what a Lean event is before proceeding. A typical Lean event is a week-long workshop that involves a cross-functional team of less than 12 employees, working together to solve a problem. Usually the in-person event is held because the solution is not known and/or the team needs to agree on the solution. This leads to intense debate and discussion among the team. In fact, the best results are achieved through respectful and intense discussions among an empowered team. This is how you transform the mind-set that prevents employees from efficiently working together (also known as breaking down organizational silos). This is how you bring people together. This is how you build culture.

In this new role as Lean coach, I realized I had a major part to play in building this culture through facilitation and empowering the team to develop the best solution. I acted as a trusted, independent party with an unbiased opinion. Sometimes, this involved challenging the team's solution with respect to the charter. Sometimes, this meant ensuring every voice on the team was heard. Sometimes, it was using a Lean tool to improve the process. I was "in charge" in the fact that I was facilitating the event but no one had to "listen" to me. I had to earn my influence as a leader and my old management style was out the window. I was on the journey and learning to see.

In the Lean world, practitioners often refer to this idea of learning to see. You use Lean tools to map the process, see waste, and make breakthrough changes in the process. By seeing the waste, you improve the process. The tools were great, but for me, learning to see became more about examining myself, observing employee interactions, and building culture. It started with improving myself and then allowed me to take lessons learned forward to coach and influence others. It's contagious and just started to spread to other parts of my life naturally.

It's hard to take a close look at yourself. I was incredibly frustrated during that first year. It was like videotaping yourself as a public speaker and watching the recording. You are uncomfortable and don't want to watch. But there is no other way to get better. I am sharing these stories because they were some of the first experiences I had where I started to "see." I was forced to look at my actions and then see the need for change. Change that only I could make and change that was not easy. When you rise to a position of leadership, you don't get there by second guessing yourself. You don't think you have weaknesses. To the contrary, you have been rewarded by opposite behaviors, such as positioning your accomplishments and showcasing your talents. In the first year of learning to see, those behaviors would need to change.

A FEW STORIES TO SHARE

Story One (The Wake-Up Call): I was used to operating independently as an experienced leader when a Gemba coach was assigned to our location. In Lean, Gemba is a Japanese term that means real place, or the place where work is done and value is added. Gemba coaches are responsible for coaching the transformation efforts on location, including the established Lean group. At that time, I had done a few events and felt confident I knew how to prep and hold the events. I had no idea what I was supposed to learn from the Gemba coach assigned to our team. I knew what I was doing. In fact, the relationship slowly started to evolve into a hate-hate relationship. The more the Gemba coach tried to teach and involve herself in the process, the more I pushed back and justified that her coaching wasn't needed. In fact, the relationship had escalated to such a poor condition that the Gemba coach added my manager to our weekly status calls. I was infuriated. But, at the end of the day, I wasn't thinking about anything I could do to make the situation better.

I cannot remember where the idea came to me. It was not the normal course of action for me to confront a person in a situation like this, but I scheduled a meeting over lunch to discuss the "situation." I was going to straighten this Gemba coach out, once and for all. I was going to put her in her place. Really? Add my manager to our status calls? Then something started to happen in the conversation as we talked. I began to see the situation differently. I began to see the Gemba coach differently. I started to listen, which evolved to learning to see.

"Why won't you let me help you?" she pleaded. The transformation had been particularly difficult from her point of view. I am sure I wasn't making it easier. Here is someone who just genuinely wanted to be part of something. She wanted to do her job and do a good job. She wanted to share the knowledge she had gained in her long career. Did I think I had nothing to learn? Did I not want to share the success from the Lean events? Did I have to do it my way? I started to see the situation differently and I felt lousy. I had nothing to lose in sharing the events and only experience and growth to gain. From then on, I started working with her in quite a different manner. We became a pair and often played off each other. I learned so much in the few months that followed before the Gemba coach departed. I had to put myself in her shoes to see her perspective and achieve the best results.

Story Two (Pull versus Push): One day, I was trying to focus on a certain issue the steering team had with regards to data. (A steering team is a team that governs Lean events in an area of work.) Data had particularly challenged the Lean transformation from the beginning of our journey. It was hard to get. Everything was hard to measure because it involved employees recording time or transactions. I drafted an analysis on my own and wanted to present it to the steering team. I was going to solve this problem. I set late-night appointments to get the steering team's time on the issue and make headway.

But with all this effort, the steering team still made no movement on the issue. I was baffled. No matter how hard I pushed, the issue just sat. In our early journey, we had an experienced Lean consultant (sensei) who would travel and advise on the Lean transformation. The sensei at the time questioned me in his slightly southern drawl, "I have no doubt that when you own something you will drive it to fruition, like a dog with a bone, but will you have their buy in?"

That moment was something I reflected on some time after it happened. That is when I came face to face with one of my best and worst qualities: tenacity. Dog with a bone. You can look it up. Merriman-Webster dictionary uses that phrase as the example after the definition. The dog held his bone with tenacity. Ironic. This was my M.O. My mode of operation was a heavy push strategy. This was the way I operated and approached everything. This was me. Being tenacious just exacerbated it.

Just to clarify, the push strategy would go something like this: "I think XYZ needs to happen and I am going to stay on it until it does." As I reflected on that comment and the situation at hand, I realized that no amount of pushing was going to resolve that situation until the team wanted to resolve it. My energy and tenacious resolve could be better spent elsewhere. That doesn't mean giving up. In fact, my "dog with a bone" behavior would not let me do that, but I would be tenacious using a pull strategy. What can I do to influence the situation in such a way that they want to do this? If it's truly the right thing to do and it's valuable for them, then it should be easy to lay the groundwork that allows them to reach their own decision and come to the same conclusion. This might mean asking the right question at the right time. This might mean letting employees speak to the situation. Maybe it's sharing a best practice. In any case, it meant being more patient and allowing them to find their way to the answer.

This was when I realized tenacity could be both a good and a bad trait. I just had to use it in the right way. By focusing on a pull strategy, it put more ownership on me to be creative at coaching and influencing the situation. I would start putting all my energy into a pull strategy. I would be tenacious at that. Tenacious at getting employee buy in. Tenacious at having the best events. Tenacious at achieving team collaboration. Tenacious by seeking out challenging events that would improve and strengthen my facilitation skills. Tenacious at coaching challenging individuals. All these areas would allow me to grow and improve my influence and leadership skills.

Story Three (Taking Feedback): One day, someone came to me, hesitantly wanting to give feedback. She was nervous but I could tell she was dying to say something. I mindfully and openly asked, "Sure, I'll take feedback." This employee proceeded to tell me that every morning when I came into work, I seemed disgruntled. In fact, I never said "hi" or "good morning." I seemed distant. My mind was somewhere else. At first, I thought, "What? I don't get it." I started to deny it but then I thought about it more. She was stating it was only the first thing in the morning. As I started to think about it, the realization hit me. I had witnessed this before. I had seen where a senior executive had passed me in the hallway. Someone I have known for years. And not even a gesture or "hello." The leader's head was somewhere else and from the receiving end, it felt totally awkward and uncomfortable. Here I was doing the same thing.

Where was my head in the morning? As a working mother of two children, mornings were the hardest part of my day. Despite my best attempt to use my Lean skills at home, getting out the door with two kids on time was stressful. There was always some drama or situation. I wasn't walking into work with a smile on my face saying, "Good morning!" My mind was still on the chaotic drop off I just had at school. My brain was still stuck in the frustration generated from the fact that my teenager wouldn't have any breakfast or my son misplaced his snow gear. The list goes on and on. One day, I was going out the door in the morning and my son was standing in the rain under the gutter where water poured down faster than other spots on the gutter. He was soaking wet. Some of the mornings were just crazy. Regardless, I realized that I was sending a wrong message to those around me just as I seen others do by not saying "hi" in the hallways. I graciously thanked the employee for her feedback. I recognized it was likely hard for her to approach me. She had to have courage. The next morning, I changed my morning routine.

It took me a little bit to get it right but I made a change. As I left the car, I cleared my brain and took a big breath. I thought about all the great qualities my kids have. My daughter is like me. She wants to change the world. She pulled together a drama club at her middle school with no dedicated teacher. Thirty students showed! My son has the same energy as me. Up in the morning and ready to go. He blazes a path in sports when he puts his mind to it and brings incredible energy to everything he does. By the time I get to the door, I am smiling. I am proud and ready for that "Good morning!"

When managed correctly, tenacity is a strength. Louis Pasteur, who is well known for changing the face of health care in his time, once said, "Let me tell you the secret that has led me to my goal. My strength lies solely in my tenacity." I share these stories as earlier examples of when I started to look at myself and where I could improve. They allowed me to learn to see and start my journey that sparked this book and many changes in my life, the first being how to use an attribute like tenacity.

BUT NOW I SEE...

Reflection kicked off this journey of self-discovery for me. I joked about it, that I was now a receiver. I was listening. To who? Everyone and anyone. And the more I did it, the more I learned things. Sometimes, they were things about myself. Sometimes, they were about how to influence others. Sometimes, they were just cool little stories. I was starting to see things in a different way. It allowed me to better navigate Lean events, conflicts, and other situations in life. Reflection brought with it a series of "aha" moments.

Given its popularity, it shouldn't be surprising that one of the first "aha" moments started with watching a TED talk by Brené Brown titled "The Power of Vulnerability." While watching this video, I realized in the stories I told earlier that I had to make myself vulnerable to start seeing where I could improve.

Let's take the discussion with the Gemba coach. I had to put my guard down to see her point of view. I was emotionally charged and ready to give it to her. I had to back down from that, do a 180-degree turn, and then consider her point of view. I had to consider that I was at fault. To me, that meant weakness at the time or putting my guard down. But, after watching Brené's TED talk, I realized it meant vulnerability or courage, although it didn't feel like courage at the time.

It was hard for me to make that change with the Gemba coach. But why? When I thought about it, what was the worst the Gemba coach could do? Leave? Yell? Big deal. Could it get any worse than it was? She had already gone to my manager about me. I realized that I didn't have as much to give up as I thought but it was courageous to me to put myself out there and put my guard down. The same conclusion worked for the other stories too. With the sensei, it was listening and being courageous enough to look at myself, realize that I was tenacious and analyze its roots in my upbringing. With the last story, it was being courageous to take feedback, own the situation, and make changes.

I could see where Brené's head was exploding as she gave that TED talk. Vulnerability is one of those words that when discussed, people cringe. Words like weakness, oversensitivity, and feebleness often accompanied it in my mind. If you walked up to someone and said, "Let's discuss your vulnerability," you might get that "deer in the headlights" look. That's how I felt. But, since I was on this journey to seeing, I was starting to figure things out for the first time in my life. Coming to terms with vulnerability meant I could put myself out there more. I could take chances. I could take risks. Then something cool came along with it.

I finally figured out what I wanted to do when I grew up. It only took me half a lifetime, but I realized I liked coaching and teaching. I should have known earlier. I should have known so many years ago. I remember being the teacher assistant my sophomore year at Purdue. The professor let me teach his class (Material and Energy Balances) a few times over the quarter. It was only 250 students to teach and I went in running. Public speaking is number one on the list of things people most fear, with death being number seven. Where the heck was my brain? I don't know. I just liked it. I was starting to have fun with it, looking externally for places to speak, teach, or coach. Sometimes using real life experiences. Sometimes using role play. I was learning to see.

In my Business Transformation role, I was doing the same thing. I was being creative in the "pull" strategy. I was figuring out how to engage employees and how to make them enthusiastic about their role at Watson Health. Again, I had fun with it! I made videos, which included my daughter as the star in a homemade video about finding waste. I took teams on field trips to our Ann Arbor neighbor, Zingerman's Mail Order, where they could explore Lean at other locations. I felt privileged to work with every team on the Lean events we had. We had awesome, creative people that rose to the challenge every time.

But, I was searching for more. I started to test my influence individually with leaders and employees I coached. My thinking was something along the lines of "everyone needs coaching so everyone has something to improve. I was always open to taking feedback in return. Why shouldn't everyone be?" I wanted everyone on the journey right alongside me.

I may have been a little overzealous at that point. I started to reach out and coach employees who crossed my path. Sometimes, it was encouraging a shy employee on their presentation skills. Sometimes, it was much bolder and involved coaching managers. It's with the latter group that I received a wide range of reactions. But as always, I had tenacity in my back pocket to hold myself strong in my resolve. I stuck with it. I just felt that we were all learners on the road to improvement, so why shouldn't I offer the perspective or feedback? I remember an older employee I had hired back in my finance days. She would often say, "We all put our pants on the same way, one pant leg at a time." No one was better or worse. They could review my feedback, reflect on their journey, and determine for themselves how they wanted to use it. In the same regard, I would gladly take feedback in return.

But if they could only see what I was seeing! I started to realize it was hard for some people to take feedback. Vulnerability? Maybe. Or maybe because everyone has their own journey, their own luggage to carry with them as well. They have their own demons to figure out and solve.

I remembered it wasn't easy for me in those earlier stories. Geez, that Gemba coach about pushed me over the edge. I ignored her for some time. Now people were sometimes ignoring me. Why? I knew. As a leader, you get to where you are based on accomplishments. Promotion comes from showing how great your work is. You don't go into an interview or ask for a promotion by saying, "Hire or promote me because I can be vulnerable" or "I can explain the last success I had. Let me tell you what I should have done better." You stack up accomplishments with no mention of vulnerability or its accompanying courage. This means though that you miss opportunities to become a better leader and to truly engage employees. Had I continued to fight the Gemba coach, I would have missed learning so much from that person in the months that followed. Had I blown off the sensei who called me a "dog with a bone," I would have missed finding the best quality about myself and more importantly, figuring out how best to use it. And had I dismissed the employee who gave me feedback about how I walked into work in the morning every day, I would have missed the opportunity to correct the simplest thing I was doing that disengaged people around me.

I wanted that for the employees I was trying to coach. I wanted them to see what I saw so they could improve. I wanted more people on the journey to seeing. Luckily, I still had tenacity in my back pocket with coaching in my sights. And then, it happened after believing long enough. I started to reach leaders. There was one leader where I remember the first time I said, "I need to give you feedback." I am sure she had never heard that before. It was not typical for our culture. Hesitantly, she said, "Yes?"

I debated: Did the "yes" end with a question as in "Okay I am not sure about this?" I think so. I was not even sure I knew her that well but off I went. I began to explain a recent experience where we were working together on a project. We had an urgent deadline and agreed on next steps. I led the action from there and coached several individuals to get the work done. Later, we met as a team and this leader completely changed direction in that meeting. My head was spinning. But worst of all, one of the individuals I had worked with on the preparation was messaging me during the meeting.

"What's going on?" "Why is she changing direction?" "Where did this come from?" Her head was spinning.

But, I was surprised and just catching up. I had no clue but I wanted to do the best by this leader and the employee. I knew leaders were pulled in a hundred thousand directions. I did my best to tell that employee, "Let's give this leader the benefit of the doubt. We need to work through this." Then I found the positive. I reinforced that the work we had done laid the groundwork for the changes this leader was now making. The work was not lost. I thanked her for working through these challenges and promised to follow up with the leader.

That employee was right though. Maybe I was sugar coating a reply to try to keep her engaged. But I knew the problem because I remembered when it happened to me as a director not so many years ago. I was meeting with an employee and asked her a bunch of questions. Reading the expression on her face, I noted something was off. Then it dawned on me and I asked, "We have gone over this before, right?" She smiled and said yes. I apologized and humbly asked for her to go over it one more time and that time I would remember. Not just remember what she told me but remember the whole story because I realized at that moment that something happens when you start getting promoted. Your focus is pulled upward and away from the work employees do. At some point in a prior meeting, my mind was probably on corporate requests or the last meeting with my boss. It hadn't been in the moment when I met with the employee.

I shared this experience with the leader as I started to give her feedback. I told her how utterly dumb I felt with that employee and that I realized it was a complete lack of focus on my part. Then I started to walk over to the experience that just happened in the recent meeting. In sharing my story, I was bringing self-awareness to her story. I could have told her what she did wrong, but who wants to hear that? It is so much more meaningful to have someone put themselves out there and learn from it.

The leader listened quietly. To her credit, she didn't defend herself, which would have been the more normal reaction. She just listened. She was on her own journey to seeing. She had to think about it and reflect on the experience. She had to process it and then decide, is there something she can do better and what is it?

I don't need her to agree with me. In fact, I don't let myself get distracted with how she or anyone reacts to the feedback. It is their journey and their choice to decide how they react and what they can change. It's tenacity that keeps me focused on my job regardless of the reactions I receive. Tenacity gives me hope that she will have that "aha" moment, start her journey and lean (no pun intended) on me as a strategic resource to help her be the best leader she can be.

Just like that, it was working. I recently met again with that same leader and after the meeting, she reached out to me and said, "Was I short in the earlier meeting?" It took me by surprise and then I realized she was listening to me and looking for feedback. I was on cloud nine. I told her that her tone was impatient and she sounded frustrated. But I knew why. She wanted the employee on the call to already be running with something.

He was asking a lot of questions, hence her frustration. Her next question was, "Do you think it was performance related?" Coaching full steam ahead.

My natural reaction again was to draw on my own experience first. I began to explain that I learned a long time ago that there were two buckets of employees: independent and structured. Independent employees are employees you can send a quick email to or have a 10-minute call with and they will go and figure out how to get the thing done. They need minimal vision and rely on themselves to brainstorm and execute. They figure out who they need to work with and complete the project or task. Structured employees are employees who require specific guidance, but once they have it, they are off and running. They require more structure but are often happy and content to do a good job with the same work. I used to think I only wanted independent employees. I am an independent employee. In fact, if you were to give me too much guidance, I would be frustrated and feel unempowered. I want challenges to figure out. While structured employees hate that idea, they can crank away on repeating work and are happy doing so. Something I would find uncomfortable and boring. The thing is you need a mixture of both.

I continued to explain this story to the leader and then told her this employee, who is frustrating you, is in the structured category. Given the logic I just explained, there is nothing wrong with that. It's not performance. Then, turning the focus back to her as the leader, I asked, "How many times have you met with the individual on this assignment? How many minutes of instruction? Any time on a one-on-one basis?" The answer came back slowly, "Not much." I explained that this employee is going to be great but is not someone who is going to read your mind. He needs structure and instruction to understand his role and then he will run with it. She thanked me. Holy smokes! She thanked me. Then she agreed to devote some time to get the employee up to speed. To engage employees, we as leaders must look to ourselves before everything else. That's where engagement starts. It starts and ends with us as leaders. Are you giving good direction? Are you listening when your employees speak? Are you creating an environment for them to succeed?

Is vulnerability contagious? I think it's the journey to seeing that is contagious. Vulnerability lets you share that journey. In these examples, it was vulnerability that allowed me to put myself out there, but in sharing my story, I helped this leader embrace her vulnerability. Vulnerability is just one of the many things to learn along the journey. A journey that is different for each one of us.

If you are thinking, "This doesn't apply to me" or "I have nothing to change, what journey?" then great! I am glad you have it all figured out. Note there is a huge smirk on my face. Why a smirk? Because unfortunately, you haven't started the journey. But if you are still listening and haven't stopped reading, I am glad you are on the journey! Your journey. It starts with reflection and I am happy to share mine if it opens the door for you. The next step is about you getting to know yourself. This is a journey of self-reflection that is yours and yours alone to make. People can give you feedback and coaching, but no one knows you as well as you know yourself. Your experience, background, and thoughts make you who you are. Your experiences and reflection will help guide you on what you want to change about yourself and how you can become more influential. Those changes are experiments. They are little things you can try. You can analyze them and impact the way you work with others. Are you composed? Are you angered? You get the idea. I encourage you to experiment as much as you can because that is where the most learning takes place.

Funny, I have been referring to myself as a "dog with a bone" when I speak about tenacity because that is what the sensei said to me at that moment. But, if I were truly honest with myself, I would probably call it something else. I am sure I could have come off as a complete bitch sometimes to get something done. I never adjusted for other personalities. I never thought about the other person's view. I wasn't looking to myself for what I could change.

But once I started to look for how to change, things just started pouring in. Ideas. Deep thoughts. Opportunities. So, let's jump to the next one. Enter compassion. Why compassion? Because compassion helps you work past conflict. A great example or place to start is a relationship with a difficult person. Think of a difficult person you know. Everyone knows someone. Maybe me before this journey. Ha. Ha. Anyway, think of that person who says something rude. Or maybe they are highly critical? Could be at home or work. It doesn't matter. They just bring some negative emotion and anger forward or frustrate you in some way. These people are great places to experiment, to learn from, and to use as practice. They don't need to know it but you can embrace them as a personal challenge.

My neighbor is a great example. She is an elderly lady and highly critical. I used to avoid her at all costs. I know I don't have my house or lawn up to her standards and guess what, I hate taking care of the lawn. If I could get my husband to move, I would in a heartbeat. We have too much lawn and too many trees, for that matter. I would prefer a condo with nothing to do. But, we have two kids, need the space, and love where we live in Michigan. You might ask, how do you know you are not up to her standards? Well, my neighbor will do not-so-subtle things like go through my backyard and kill poison ivy only to tell me about it, stating that my kids are now protected. Or maybe it's a gift, like a gallon of mildew remover that hints to the fact that our fence is turning green by her house. It doesn't matter that she has a ton of garbage in that same area. It doesn't matter that

I hate the tarps she throws up in her backyard every winter. She has decided in her head what is wrong and right. The stuff she does is good. The things I do are "not so good." You can likely hear a little emotion building in my voice as I write. It's a little more than annoying.

I started to look at her as an opportunity to better my skills. An opportunity for what? To practice calmness, mindfulness, and compassion. You need to believe first that emotion or reacting is something you wish to avoid. Difficult people naturally elicit this response, but when you are reacting, you are not mindful and can miss opportunities around you, even with a neighbor. If you are still reflecting on what the difficult person did that angered you, you are not in the present moment. If you don't like that idea, just think of it as a place to practice your composure. Compassion lets you do that. I now think about her first as someone's mom, someone's grandma. She means well. Her intentions are good despite the delivery. This compassionate line of thinking softens my view point in the conversation.

My friends think I'm crazy especially when I talk about my favorite story. It starts with a lawn full of scattered brown spots. I remember jogging one day on the way back to the house. I saw the spots and slowed my run. I was thinking, "Maybe we have grubs? Wonder what's going on here?" We have never had brown spots and then subtly, my neighbor approached me. Leading with "I'm sorry," she began to explain that she had gotten quite upset one day. We had a neighbor across the street from both of us who would let their weeds go. The seeds often rolled on to her lawn and caused constant weeds. That neighbor moved and the new owner put new grass in. It was a dream for her. There would be no more weeds. Except a few pesky weeds were still festering at the end of my lawn. Given we hardly did anything with our lawn, the weeds grew and were now sending seeds to her lawn. Her dream was shattered and in a fit of anger, she stormed over to my lawn to kill the weeds. In her haste though, she accidentally grabbed grass killer instead of weed killer. She apologized but naturally, had I done something about the weeds in the first place, she wouldn't have had to do that.

I know most of the men reading this book are gasping, "She touched your lawn?" Yeah, she touched my lawn and here she was confessing but with the caveat that it was my fault given I had let the weeds persist. Enter compassion. I look at my neighbor the way I want others to look at my mom. I want them to give her a break because she struggles through her daily life ever since my dad passed away. I am sure she drives people crazy. Maybe at the drive-thru as she loudly shouts her food order. Maybe at a restaurant because she changes her mind a hundred times on the order. Maybe at a local shop because she is lonely and just wants to talk to someone. She will start a whole conversation about anything. I hope that compassion is there for her.

Thinking of it in that way lets me respond to this neighbor with, "No big deal. It'll grow back." My friends think I am crazy for not telling her off. The world has so little love in it. I think we can change that. So, she killed part of my lawn and then blamed me for it. I can have broad enough shoulders to let that fly.

Emotion, except when used to inspire or energize people, is a weakness. It leads to overreaction or not giving the other person the benefit of the doubt. The opposite of compassion. It decreases your influence and leads to missed opportunities. It leads to nothing except frustration within yourself. Don't believe me? Let me share a few examples.

My job is such that I am supposed to be frank and tell people when things are going wrong. I am supposed to challenge them on what they need to fix. Sometimes I forget that not everybody is as comfortable talking about something going wrong, especially when it's in an area they own. I view it as the process is broken and has nothing to do with the person involved. But for the person involved, it can be extremely emotional and cause him or her to lash out or feel disengaged. I remember one email I sent. There were two areas for Lean improvement taking place and I thought they might overlap. I sent an email to the leaders involved, pointing this out and asking them to work it out. Within minutes, I had this emotional email stating that the email I had sent earlier was a "slap in the face." Within hours, that leader had gone to my boss, without talking to me directly. Without giving me the benefit of the doubt. Without trying to see my point of view. No compassion but a lot of emotion. I wondered about that incident for some time. Did this leader really think I was intending to be mean? Did she really think I was coming in to slap her and her staff around? When you take a step back, it's so silly. But this leader was buried in emotion. I did do my part. I took a step back and reflected on the email. I showed the email to a trusted colleague and asked if it was too strong. Was it insulting? A puzzled look only followed. In the end, I just let the whole thing go. However, the leader missed something. She never understood the point to my email. A missed opportunity due to something so silly.

In fact, if you as a leader are experiencing any negative emotion (overreaction, frustration, hurt, etc.), you are disengaging someone somewhere. One of my events involved a leader where her process was being examined in the Lean event. The metrics were bad. Poor quality and throughput. Hard for any leader to own, and I had compassion for that leader. If I had been in that spot, I would have felt the same way. During the first day, the team was doing what I thought they should be doing: examining current state, which meant reflecting on how the current process was performing. Poorly. Not being mean. Just honest and the data showed it. We needed to be able to talk through what was currently taking place before we could examine how to fix them. To me, it felt like every other event, but as I left the building that night, my phone lit up. My gut sunk as I thought, "What the heck?" There was a whole exchange of conversation about the first day of the event taking place among executives outside the event. The leader in the event was upset. She was frustrated and noted that she would not be at the event the next morning.

Every bone in my body wanted to call her up and tell her to go take a flying leap. But I will stop there. I already told you nothing becomes of emotion used in a negative way. Compassion means I need to put myself in her shoes. I am sure the first day of looking at poor performance was hard to take. After several messages, we decided to meet at 7:00 a.m. the next morning. She came in ready to walk away. I mustered every thought of servant leadership I had. (Servant leadership refers to the nontraditional leadership style, where the leader puts the needs of others first and helps people develop and perform as highly as possible.) I reminded myself: I am in this position to serve. I recited a quote by Alan Mullaly from Ford to myself several times over: "At the heart of it, it's an honor to serve." "It's an honor to serve." Maybe just one more. "It's an honor to serve." Just a side note, I often say quotes from people or movies to help stay positive and focused. With tenacity in my back pocket, I met with that leader and, with the quote gently reciting in the back of my brain, I opened my mind and heart and comfortably listened.

The leader recounted some comments by fellow teammates. She found them harsh. I apologized. It was my job as facilitator to fend off nasty comments. I didn't think it was particularly negative but if she felt this way, I missed something and it was my fault. Then the leader noted that she wanted time in the day to present her upcoming changes. And again, I apologized, telling her that current state usually comes first but we had time in the agenda as the team approached future state.

Then I did what I do best. I have coined it often as my soap box speech. I pick a theme or goal and, in my mind, I get up on a soap box and use all the positive emotion and energy I have to passionately speak to that theme. In this case, the goal was to get that leader back in the room and without issue. The rest of the team had no idea what was going on. Heck, half of them had told me the night before what a great event it was. If she left, it wouldn't be good for her. It wouldn't be good for the team. It wouldn't be good for Lean. No good would come from letting her leave as is.

So, up on the soap box I went and my brain unloaded on reasons. You as the leader need to be part of the event for it to be successful. You can't blame the team. They are reacting to the metrics. They won't feel different about your group or your improvements until the data changes. I noted positive comments that team members had made the night before. I noted changes I would make to ensure day two would not repeat the same experience for her. I likely groveled. "At the heart of it, it's an honor to serve." She decided to come back to the Lean event the next day and finished her time. Tenacity, you rock!

But it wasn't tenacity alone. It started with compassion. If it were my broken process and colleagues were speaking honestly about it, I would have felt the same way. Anyone would really. It was compassion that had me talk her back into the event. It was the best thing for her. How could I have explained her leaving? How would the team have been able to accomplish anything without her involvement? She owned the process. She had to be there.

But even though I am on this journey of seeing, it does not mean I don't make mistakes. I completely own the fallout from the event. My job is to make sure that everyone feels comfortable and I missed something on that first day or more likely in the prep. But what struck me so profoundly about this incident was the emotion and lack of compassion. This leader acted as if I intentionally just let other managers bash her over the head. This leader acted as if I was completely incompetent in my facilitation. This leader reacted and let all her emotion out, without giving me one ounce of compassion. Laura means well. I trust Laura. Laura knows her skill. Not there. In fact, it was the complete opposite powered by a lot of emotion. Then, ironically, I had to suck up every bit of emotion I had about the event and talk the leader back into participating. When the team later remarked how valuable her participation was, I smiled and acted like nothing had happened. "At the heart of it, it's an honor to serve." Taking myself out of it, what's important is that the event improved things greatly for those involved, and that is servant leadership.

We are only human. I have just as many emotions as that leader but now when those emotions come, I know my energy is better spent elsewhere, which brings us to mindfulness. If emotions are racing, you cannot possibly be present. I usually explain mindfulness using a fun hobby of mine, triathlons. Beyond the energy in the race, what attracts me to triathlons is that the race tests you on mindfulness. It is an awesome race that requires you to focus on the moment. How so? The story I love to tell is of one race in South Haven, Michigan. While racers were energized and setting up their equipment, I came in with my gear and bike. I was diligently going over my prep (food, goggles, sunglasses, hat, etc.), when the racer next to me started talking about the wetsuit debate. It's almost always a topic for discussion and goes something like this: You can't wear a wetsuit above 78 degrees Fahrenheit, but when the temperature is below that, it is your decision as the racer. The wetsuit makes you faster because of buoyancy so most want to wear it, but it can be a pain in the butt to take off. If you don't practice these transitions, it can be intimidating. Obviously, when it's cold you wear it, but when it's close to 78 but not quite 78, it becomes a debate. I decided to wear the wetsuit. I had practiced and thought it would go okay. I hated being cold. The wetsuit would keep me warm as we waited on the beach for the start of the race. The racer next to me said he would rough it. It was in the transition area that our paths crossed again, between biking and running. He was bothered and mumbled to me that he should have worn the wetsuit. Hurriedly, he went off as I was taking a few extra seconds to make sure I didn't forget anything. I noticed something but couldn't yell fast enough or loud enough. He took off running in the wrong lane. He went out the "in" shoot versus the "out" shoot. The wrong direction but it was too late. He was fast and gone.

Mindfulness is being present. It's about grounding yourself in the exact moment so you avoid mistakes or more importantly, act on opportunities. It's not about what just happened and not about where you are going, but right now. This exact moment.

Are you reading this book? Or are you thinking about what you need to do tomorrow? Or are you still mad about something that happened earlier today? It's about staying in this moment right now and making the most of it. You get the idea. You already decided what you are going to do with this moment. In this case, read my book. Thank you. But, then do the best you can with it. Learn from it and don't be distracted. It goes like this for anything really. A meeting. A drop-by conversation. Checking out at the grocery store. Every minute is an opportunity to learn. Every minute is an opportunity to see something. Every minute you can make a difference in someone's life. That's how you change engagement and earn influence as a leader. Notice I say earn. Position doesn't make you a leader with employees. Calling the shots or a fancy office. Being engaged drives engagement and for that, you need mindfulness.

"My contributions are not valued," flashed on my computer as a message. "That doesn't sound good," I thought. I replied to the employee in my usual inquisitive tone, "Hey, what's up? What are you thinking?" This employee was on one of my Lean teams and we were working on improvements. The leader in charge of the workstream had set up the invite and mistakenly left her off the invite in her haste. A small minor mistake any leader could make, right? The flipside. Such a large feeling of disengagement it meant for this employee.

Mindfulness and compassion are so important in our lives. Mindfulness is important because leaders have the obligation to be better than this. Servant leadership. "It's an honor to serve." We earn that right and we do it with every choice we make in each moment. Compassion is important because we all need to bend and give the other person the benefit of the doubt. In this case, the leader was busy and missed including this employee. Not an excuse but we are all human and anyone could make that mistake. Was that employee on the team just as guilty? Why jump all the way to not being valued? Why not just give the leader the benefit of the doubt and know your value? Culture is finding mechanisms that let you bend toward each other. Both need to reflect on what they can do better and where they can improve.

It's mindfulness that lets me be the receiver I called myself earlier. I can't explain it other than being in the moment and focused on what is going on in that moment. Then an opportunity or idea presents itself. Sometimes it is triggered by a totally odd thing, but it is up to me to pluck it from that moment and then do something with it. This book is a great example. Where did the idea to write this book come from? I was at the Michigan Lean Consortium year-end conference. Zingerman's Mail Order had donated their dynamite chocolate chip cookies and sitting right next to it was this cute, fun book, titled "Zingerman's Guide to Giving Great Service." Idea received. Wonder if I could write a book like this? Then I started, and it evolved from a fun little book about Lean to a personal journey, which now you are reading. And that's how it works. I have a ton of examples like this. Things I would have missed had I not been fully engaged in the moment. Mindfulness and curiosity allowed me to find my purpose in life and a new kind of happiness.

FINDING PURPOSE

I mentioned I loved to coach, teach, and speak publicly. Again, in being tenacious, I was focusing on being the best Lean coach I could be. What this meant to me was growth. If I grew my skills, I would have more to offer the team whether it was conflict resolution, brainstorming, or problem-solving. Eleanor Roosevelt once said, "Do one thing every day that scares you." She was one of my personal heroes and that quote resonated with me. I started with looking for places to put myself out there. I was searching for ways to challenge myself. Sometimes it was reaching out to someone I admired, and then I would make my way to make an introduction. Sometimes I was teaching. Sometimes I was volunteering. And sometimes I was signing up for speaking opportunities. With speaking, it was something extra special that drew me to that. I wasn't just presenting off a PowerPoint, I was searching for ways to engage the audience, such as doing a role play exercise or something a little crazy. I wasn't exactly sure why I was doing it, but it was fun and helped me grow as a Lean coach.

About that time, I attended a conference, and the presenter covered growth using three concentric circles, or 3 zones: comfort zone (inner circle), learning zone (middle circle), and danger zone (outer zone). The instructor explained how most people liked to operate within the comfort zone. Makes sense. That's what you know. The instructor further went on to explain that to learn and grow, you needed to be able to leave the comfort zone. You needed to take a risk and venture out into the outer rings. In doing that, you learn and you grow. I realized that is what I had been doing under Mrs. Eleanor Roosevelt's advice. I was putting myself out there and looking for challenges in public speaking, facilitating difficult people, or having complex problems to solve. The harder, the better. That meant I was growing. I hadn't thought about it in in this fashion, but I started to understand it using this framework.

I was focused on growth, which improved my skills. Great! But something was still missing. Something was still eluding me. I was still searching for the why. Why do all this? I could just as easily be sitting at home watching a TV series or shopping. Sometimes I would watch people who liked to just chill and do nothing. Why was I always going? As my husband would often comment at different points, "Why take on all this extra stuff? You're nuts." Was I taking on too much? It just felt natural and good to me. It was my work but it was also my hobby and what I just plain enjoyed doing.

Then the answer came. It was mindfulness in a Design Thinking workshop that would bring me the answer. I was sitting in the workshop, reviewing a ton of tools with the instructor, when one tool caught my eye. It was called the Purpose Map. Ok, I must have loved concentric circles. The Purpose Map was yet another set of three concentric circles.

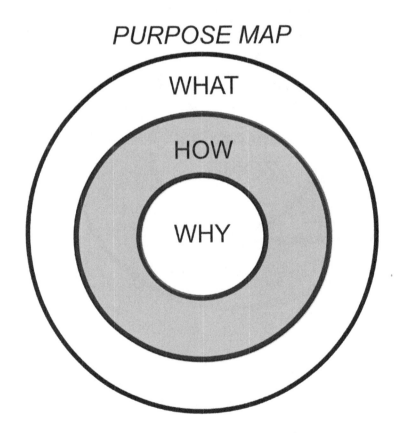

PURPOSE MAP

WHAT

HOW

WHY

But, there was something about it. In Design Thinking, it was a framework to determine your purpose as a business. I was sitting in the class, when it struck me that I could use this same framework to examine my purpose. In a way, I already had it filled out. The outer ring was the "what." The "what" for me was transformation. Transforming or changing anything really. Making things better at work through Lean events. Sharing knowledge with fellow colleagues and transforming their thinking. Or presenting to students and transforming their frame of mind. Building better leaders. In the end, I loved to make someone's life better.

The middle ring was the "how." How would I do this? Through coaching events. Through public speaking. Through networking. Through teaching. But the "why" at the center ring was still escaping me.

I remember the instructor saying most companies know the "what" and the "how" but not the "why." Yeah, that sounded familiar. For a company, the purpose map brought all three things (what, how, and why) together in a statement that supported the company's mission. I reflected on the awesome mission for Watson Health: "To improve lives and give hope by delivering innovation to address the world's most pressing health challenges through data and cognitive insights."

Nothing better than that. Then it hit me. The why for me was "inspire." Inspire. I repeated it. It felt right but sounded so weird. It sounded like I was just this mythical muse that floated around carrying ideas and knowledge. Music would play in the background as ideas fell from the heavens. But when I looked to my role in events, that kind of was me. I was listening and contributing where I felt it made the most sense for the team to progress. But inspire what? Many people thought of tools when it came to the Lean events: A3 thinking, Kanban, visual management, mapping, etc. Sure, I used that stuff, but I was much more interested in how to empower and engage employees. Why? Because if they were truly engaged, the improvements would sustain, and not only sustain but evolve into their culture. At the heart of it, that's what mattered the most to me. As I thought about it, "bold" popped into my head. I say "bold" change because in Lean events, I pushed the teams not to settle for status quo. Not to settle for the way things have always been. To use all their talents and unleash creativity. To take a step back and say, "Is this the process you would set up if this was your own business?" Just like that, the "why" and the eventual name of this book— "Inspiring Bold" —were born.

MY PURPOSE

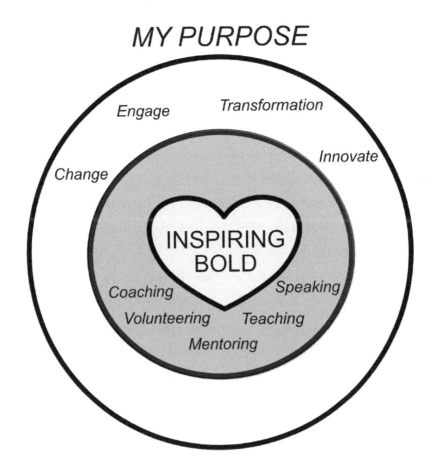

Just like how Watson Health has its awesome mission, I thought I should have an awesome mission too. I wanted to know how my "why" fit into what Watson Health was doing. A "how do I fit" mission statement. What was that? I wasn't sure at first. I loved the awesome stories about cancer patients and who we helped. It was truly incredible what Watson Health was doing but those people seemed so far away from what I was doing. How do I save lives? How do I fit in? How do I help the patients and the person at the end of the process? And then it came to me: "Saving lives by inspiring bold change and improving the daily work our Watson Health employees do!" All this just started becoming part of who I was. It was my why at work and aligned with my passion as a human being.

I was starting to connect the dots. I started to realize that my job, coaching in events, was like a sandbox to play in and learn new things. Why? Because they naturally produced conflict, and not just any type of conflict. Intense concentrated human conflict. Not in a bad way, but that was just the nature of the Lean events. The team gelled and formed as they worked through the problem they were given to solve. We often referred to the Elizabeth Kübler-Ross diagram when starting events because the change curve was exactly what teams experienced. Elizabeth Kübler-Ross was a psychiatrist who studied people with terminal illness. In her book, "On Death and Dying," she outlined five stages that dying patients experienced: denial, anger, bargaining, depression, and acceptance. I would often refer to the curve as the "valley of despair."

Every team I had on a Lean event went through the "valley of despair" and experienced these similar stages. They would start with examining current state and a related problem to solve. Shock. Denial. Anger. These emotions came forward as the team grounded themselves in where they were starting. They were coming to terms with how bad things currently were. Then as the team worked on the problem and collaborated on solutions, out of the "valley of despair," they came with a whole set of new emotions. Acceptance. Commitment. Enthusiasm. Engagement.

"VALLEY OF DESPAIR"

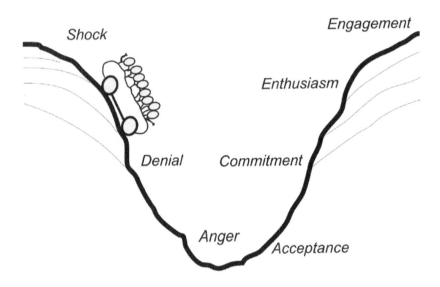

I had never thought of myself as a student of behavior, a phrase commonly thrown around for reflecting on these human interactions, but that is what I was doing. I was learning from the teams. I was learning from the leaders and I was learning from myself. It wasn't just facilitating and coordinating an agenda. It was dissecting a behavior and determining how to interact with that behavior to win it over. It was evaluating interactions and using my influence to help guide those interactions into collaboration. It was a true place to inspire people and to inspire bold breakthrough change. Employee engagement at its best. Then better yet, I found that being vulnerable again and courageous enough to talk about these experiences helped influence others on their journey. It helped them to "see."

I often tell the gorilla story, which wraps this up quite nicely. I was facilitating a Lean event and did not realize one of the team members had been on another Lean event about six months prior. The employee had a miserable experience in that earlier event. He noted it on our event survey that we hand out after events. He described the entire experience. He felt steamrolled at times by stronger personalities in the room. He felt his voice wasn't heard. He thought it was a terrible process. He never made it out of the "valley of despair." I didn't know any of that though because I wasn't the facilitator at the earlier event. As the team started working through the issue, it evoked a deep discussion on how to solve one of the problems. It was one of the tougher events I had because the team was evenly divided. We hated to make solutions by voting. Voting really isn't true collaboration because those who lose the vote are not always bought in. This employee was having a hard time getting a word in edgewise. I could feel his frustration as the stronger personalities ignored team rules like, "Every voice counts."

Then I remembered something the Gemba coach had said to me and I never thought I would have to use it. She talked about a talking stick, and as that advice came rushing back in my head, I picked up a spoon by the table with food and called it the "talking spoon." I explained to the team that they could only speak if they had the spoon in their hand. Some scoffed at first or chuckled at me. I was being vulnerable in putting myself out there but I didn't let the laughter faze me. I had tenacity in my back pocket and was not going to let them speak unless they had the spoon in their hand. After a few more chuckles and some corrections to the rule, the team had become accustomed to talking only with the talking spoon in hand. It slowed down the stronger personalities in the room and allowed quieter employees to have a voice. It allowed the whole team more time to process and fostered a meaningful discussion. I spent the next four tiring hours running around a room like an idiot and handing the spoon from person to person. Those same personalities who were laughing at me in the beginning were now eagerly waiting their turn like schoolchildren with their hands raised in a classroom. The experience changed that employee. He had hated the process and now saw something so different. Maybe it was me putting myself out there. In the beginning, I was letting the team have fun at my expense. Maybe it was me running around like a crazy person. But I think it's because I cared enough to do that and that employee knew it.

He is now one of the strongest Lean advocates we have and approaches me with enthusiastic ideas all the time. So where is the gorilla in all this, right? How does that tie into vulnerability and courage? Well, one day this same employee approached me in the lunch room and said, "Laura, I have the best idea!" I mindfully listened as he started to enthusiastically explain that he appreciated knowing about the "valley of despair" on that first day. It was helpful to know that the Lean events could be that intense and that was just part of the process. Because of that, he suggested we have someone dressed in a crazy gorilla suit walk into the room at the team's toughest point, their "valley of despair." Why? To lighten the mood. To bring the team up. To engage and have some fun. It was a great idea and although our Lean team has yet to coordinate that surprise for future Lean events, I was able to do something else with the idea and the whole experience. Mindfulness. Plucking the idea from the moment. I decided to share this story with others at the first breakout session I did for Michigan Lean Consortium (MLC). I partnered with a colleague and named it, "They call it facilitating, but we call it FUN!" As the title implied, it seemed natural to start the session with doing something fun. Insert gorilla story with a bit of acting. At the beginning of the session, my colleague was hiding in the bathroom with a gorilla mask as I proceeded to act extremely frustrated that he was late. I was role playing. Why? Why not? It was something I hadn't done. Vulnerability. It seemed like it would make a fun spectacular entrance. Courage. As I continued to show frustration, I remember one of the attendees, remarking, "Hey, isn't this supposed to be the fun session?" I think he was worried that I was upset. It turns out my acting wasn't half bad. I moved on and asked who was holding the banana. One of the participants at the table raised the banana and my colleague in the gorilla suit came rushing in, with actual gorilla noises and all.

With all eyes staring at the both of us, I then explained how the gorilla was a fun ice breaker. More importantly, this story about the talking spoon is about engaging and reaching every employee. What are you willing to do to get just one more person on the transformation journey to change? Run around like a nut with a spoon in my hand. Easy. It was showing a little vulnerability in taking the chance to use the spoon. I didn't care if people laughed. That was better. Lighten the mood at my expense. No worries. But that gesture and willingness to serve meant something to that employee. It meant all the difference in the event to him and it meant something to me. I was inspired and more determined than ever to Inspire Bold at Watson Health. Tenacity still in my back pocket, I remember thinking, "One at a time, if that's what it takes."

Being on the journey to seeing meant one eye-opening moment after another. Again, I was a receiver. I was reflecting on things and then seeing an opportunity. Sometimes I knew exactly what to do with them. Other times, I had to think about it for some time. Something had bugged me so many years ago when my dad died. I remembered what my mom said after my dad's death: "Dad always said you'd give the shirt off your back to anyone who asked." At the time, it struck me as odd. I wasn't in the peace corps. I wasn't working for a charity. That wasn't me but it was me when I was young. I remembered doing things like extra chores as a kid. Sometimes I would just vacuum the house for my mom. Sometimes I was helping a neighbor with their leaves. Didn't matter what, I just wanted to be helpful, with nothing in return.

It was mindfulness again that would teach me a lesson. I was sitting in my son's Tae Kwon Do class when I noticed a quote written on the whiteboard: "Burnout is not about giving too much of yourself. It's about trying to give what you do not possess." I was struck with this overwhelming feeling that maybe that thing my dad said was just to redirect me to giving what I had to give. I had been burned out and not exactly sure where I was going. Maybe I was focused on the wrong things. Stature. Title. Caught up constantly in the day-to-day grind of both work and life and focused on me. Or what I wanted or maybe where I thought I should be? Maybe I just needed to give what I had? Just like when I was little.

I had already started down that path. Maybe it was vulnerability or compassion that softened me and redirected my purpose. But I was putting myself out there to help and if it was tied to my purpose, I was there. Sometimes without even knowing it. I had been mentoring a colleague as part of the Women of Watson Health Ann Arbor Mentorship Program. She was looking for career advice but as I asked more questions, she revealed that she had been told her department was being disbanded. She was looking for another position and really wanted to stay with Watson Health.

Tenacity? You bet. I was determined to help her. It was just a matter of making the right connection. I thought of as many things as I could. A laundry list of things for her to do. Don't get me wrong. She had to do the work, but I was giving her ideas or a different perspective given my experience. Sometimes it was an introduction. A manager who was hiring. An employee she could ask about his or her position. Or a person who had been with IBM for a long time and might have another perspective to give. She enthusiastically followed up on everything I brought forward. She thanked me repetitively, and I remember saying at some point, "I was just giving what I had to give."

In highlighting the mentorship program, this colleague shared her story in a Women of Watson Health blog. She described the process and my role in detail, "Before signing up for this program, my team members and I received some news that our department would lose our jobs at the end of June. With Laura knowing my situation she jumped into gear helping wherever she could. First, we scheduled weekly meetings anywhere from fifteen minutes to an hour depending on our availability. No matter how much time was available, she always made me feel like I was the priority. Next, we discussed my career path and where I wanted to go within the company. From there she put me in contact with so many people, which really helped with networking and it got my name out there. Each meeting she gave me mini assignments, from reaching out to various people throughout the company, revamping my resume, practicing interview questions, etc. Through this journey it has revitalized something in me and has given me hope that I can and I will succeed!"

I did something special for this employee. I gave her help. I gave her inspiration and helped her believe in herself. But you know what, any leader could have done it. Any leader could have helped her with her resume or interview practice. Any leader could have helped her network. They just had to be present. They just had to give. Just like the quote from Tae Kwon Do, I would give what I had to give and do so freely.

I don't know if this is getting too deep, but I found the universe has a way of giving back when you do that. Not always, but the more I put myself out there by giving, taking chances, or learning, the more opportunities the universe shows me. This book is a great example. I would have never guessed a year ago I would be publishing anything. Writing was something I loved to do as a kid and yet I drifted far away from it. Just like drifting away from giving and helping people. Every time I turn around now, I am writing in my journal and already coming up with the next thing. It's been this willingness to give where I could around my purpose without thinking about where it was going that has brought me the best connections and opportunities in this last year.

Don't believe me? Here is another great example. I have helped out a professor at the University of Michigan by speaking at some of her classes. It was a safe place for me to test my material and grow my public speaking skill. One time, she asked me to participate on a career panel. I was not in the mood. I had a lot going on with the kids that week but my husband said, "Go ahead! It's a great opportunity!" He is always great with all this crazy stuff I do. But I still wasn't in the mood, so I asked everyone on our team in Ann Arbor but no one could make it. Reflecting on my purpose, I asked myself, "Is this not my purpose? Am I not here to inspire? And if not college students, then who?" So, I went.

Now here is the weird thing. I had mentioned I liked to participate in triathlons as a hobby. This is my personal interest. If I haven't been vulnerable enough in writing this book so far, this next story will be the ultimate test. Unlike other races, most triathlons have a weight class. Let me say that again, ladies. Most triathlons have a weight class. When you sign up, you can pick Athena for women or Clydesdale for men. The minimum range for Athena is anywhere from 145 to 160lbs. I had raced for several years, knowing my time would take first place if I only picked the Athena class. But I had such a stigma in my head about it. As the ladies reading this book know, there is nothing more vulnerable than putting your weight out there for the whole world to see. But I was soul searching. Why couldn't I sign up year after year? Why couldn't I be proud of winning that class?

Triathlons are hard events, and carrying extra weight compared to some of the string beans racing is also hard and deserves recognition. Then in the last race, I signed up for the Athena class.

I took first place in a triathlon at South Haven, Michigan. I stayed for the awards ceremony at the end and bashfully walked up to get my prize in front of a ton of much thinner athletes. I was proud. It dawned on me later that this made a great story and belonged somewhere. But where? Then I found it. Dove soap. Dove often featured women as part of their Real Beauty campaign. I would just reach out to them and give them the story. Simple, right? But I couldn't figure out where online to submit it.

At this point you are probably wondering, what does all this have to do with University of Michigan and the career panel? Well, I didn't want to go that night. I was tired and just wanted to veg out at home. Do nothing. But I listened to my purpose and went. Giving what I had to give. Advice. One of the three other panelists happened to work for Unilever, who makes Dove soap. Unbelievable, right? He worked at the plant in northwest Indiana. I waited patiently until the presentations were over. There were a ton of students still asking questions at the end. The two of us were the last ones left with several students. He could tell I wanted to ask something. And as he looked me, I said, "Well I was just waiting, because I had a question for Unilever, or Dove really." So that was it, I had him and the students staring at me, dying to know what the question was.

"Geez, do I need to give the whole same story again?" What the heck. Inquiring minds wanted to know. If I was willing to share it with Dove, why not share it with these students? I told the story. When I was done, with inquisitive young faces still staring, he looked at me with a smile, and said just that morning the Dove brand folks had visited his plant and he would connect me. He turned to the students and remarked, "That's how it's done." It was funny karma. Now I am not yet on a Dove commercial.

But the point is if I had passed on the opportunity to talk to those students, I would have never connected with this individual who then helped me with something I just happened to be working on. I was giving what I could give on something completely unrelated and getting something back in return.

I was starting to say things like, "I love my job." There was something particularly invigorating about how all this was connecting. I was reflecting on myself and what I could do better, especially with my good friend, tenacity. I had learned things like vulnerability, compassion, and mindfulness and was looking to learn and practice more. I had found my purpose and knew I was making dad proud. I was seeing opportunities presented to me and giving where I could. A bold job at a bold company. Nothing better but that doesn't mean it would always be easy.

IT'S HARDER THAN IT SOUNDS...

Even with knowing all this, it was still hard for me to be a servant leader at times. Human nature? Maybe. But there is also something to be said for the type of leaders we are developing. In my journey, it took some hard moments to shake up how I was operating. But it was often my old behavior that was rewarded and now I was looking at things differently, with the lofty idea that serving others would later present me with better opportunities. Too altruistic? Maybe, but it's something about staying with what you love. Things can try to draw you away from that. I had been teaching a class on Lean Leadership at Oakland University in Rochester, Michigan, and thought I had found the perfect book to use. The book covered leadership principles but the company where the author worked also did tours. I reached out to the author and asked, "Hey, if I have the students buy your book, would you consider the tour for free?" I was trying to keep the costs down for the students. I was all excited and then the reply came: "I'll have to charge you. Hope you understand."

No. I don't understand. My fast finance brain did the quick math, $800. It was a write-off. I was annoyed. So, I submitted the syllabus, with an article in place of the book, and decided to take the students on tour somewhere else. I likely was reacting, but it reminded me so much of something that happened to me when I was in high school.

I tried out for the high school swimming team. I swam all the time. Never took a lesson. Who would have known, I had a killer breast stroke. Didn't know half the other strokes but I would zoom in the breast stroke races. So fast that I made Varsity my freshman year. And yes, the seniors on the team without the Varsity jackets loved me. I am being sarcastic. It was horrible. I was shunned and not equipped with how to deal with it. That experience took something I loved to do (swimming) and made me hate it. I gave up. I realized at that point that I always wanted this to be about the giving and not the receiving. Leave the "what's in it for me" behind.

But despite all these feelings of altruism, I still had to work at it. I remember a project where I volunteered to help. Let me repeat that word. Volunteered. In the first few planning sessions, I struggled with where the project was going. It felt to me all over the place. A lot of ideas but no framework. Sometimes feedback was shot down and later resurfaced in another manner. It wasn't just me. I knew someone else on the team was equally frustrated in the same way.

So maybe it's the natural problem solver in me, but I tried to put together a framework, which was quickly shot down but then reused in parts. My inner guts were just annoyed. I felt like quitting the project. Why did I sign up for this? Then I started to wonder why this was bugging me so much and bugging my friend on the team. What was important here? It was important for the project to be successful. Then I tried to put myself in the project leader's shoes. I didn't think the project leader had led this type of project before but she surely doesn't want to be second guessed or challenged. It's not my place to disagree with the way the project leader is running it. I am a volunteer. It's my place to give ideas and help with tasks where I have capacity to do so.

Funny, this is how I always acted in the Lean events. There, my role was clear. I was an outside influence and coach to the team, raising challenges and giving ideas. I never got wrapped up in how they used them. But here outside of my Lean role, it was so easy to slip back into old habits. I wanted a thank you. I wanted credit for something. Anything. But it wasn't there. It was that wretched enemy, ego, that was causing me unease.

The next chance I had, I told my friend on the team that we were there for ideas and collaboration. The project leader was in charge and if the project was successful, it didn't matter whose idea was used where or how the project evolved as we worked on it. My friend was not as convinced. I wondered why. Lean had started me on this journey of self-awareness. What this meant to me in situations like these was putting my ego aside, but in a normal world, few people did this. Most started from the world of "I." Most didn't even know it.

I understood this for some time. I would sit in meetings and someone would present. Sometimes it felt like a constant barrage of "I's." I think this. My vision is this. I put together this. And so on and so on. Sometimes I would count the "I" references—how many times did the person refer to themselves in the first person? In what amount of time? It became a little bit of a game in my head. What's your "I-per-minute" ratio? Quite interesting.

Now I know you are probably asking yourself, "Well you just wrote this whole book in the first person," and you would be correct. To be honest, when I started, I found it hard to do. It felt boastful but I couldn't figure out how else to write it. It is a personal journey after all.

Let me give you the most perfect example of this I can. I had a Lean event where one of the team members came up to me at least seven times during the event, saying, "I just want to make a difference, Laura, that's all." Great statement on the face of it, right? But it annoyed me. Why was it so annoying? It was the "I." Why does it have to be "I"? Why not "we"? "We just need to make a difference" works just as well. Or one level better, "This team is going to make the difference." This is how I tried to talk. At first it was hard but then it became habit. Even if someone asked me my opinion, I tried to take the "I" out of it. I would say, "There are two things to consider..." or "Crucial to the success is..." When you start practicing this, at first it's hard. You catch the "I's" pop up and correct them. Then you learn there are so many ways of saying something without using the first person.

So why the "I"? There are many reasons one could give. Culture. Habit. Human nature. When you start thinking of truly practicing servant leadership, to me what you need to let go of is ego. The same ego I let surface in the volunteering story. Why did I try and jump in? Why did I need a thank you? Why did I want credit?

As I was building this material into the curriculum of my class at Oakland University, I thought this example was a great way to demonstrate servant leadership. But then I wondered, will someone ask me if you are not using "I" or not concerned about the credit, then how do you get promoted? Valid question after all. In today's world, I imagine this is also naturally behind the "I". "I want to make a difference" translates to "I want to do something that gets me visibly recognized and presents further opportunity." I can't argue with this because in a company where servant leadership does not reign, likely these are the vehicles and methods by which you get promoted. I have also been there.

Even today, I might throw out an idea that people love. It gets traction and then I find myself wondering about the credit, but I always bring my focus back to what's important: the improvement being made. The project at hand. This is what makes it hard but I can offer a few thoughts about it.

I choose confidence. I choose to believe in the unique value I bring. In knowing that, the value speaks for itself. I don't have to do anything extra to build it up or draw attention to it. My efforts would be better used in focusing on other opportunities or areas where I can develop. By doing this, I concentrate on growing myself and it's this growth that will lead to other opportunities I want. Getting sucked into the politics of positioning distracts you from building your value. The leader I want to work for realizes the difference.

I also choose mindfulness. Letting your mind wander in the politics of how things look and who gets credit means you are caught up in other things instead of the moment at hand. Our minds are such powerful tools. They take in information and form whole scenarios before we know it. This can weigh us down and cause us to miss opportunities right in front of us. What I am suggesting is to focus every bit of energy you have around what you are about (purpose) and how you find your way there (growth), and give people the benefit of the doubt (compassion). In that way, detractors, like need for getting credit, disappear. A bit altruistic? Perhaps. But accompanying altruism is happiness, and it doesn't get better than that. If you truly believe people have the best intentions, you give them leeway and put your thoughts and feelings aside. This is the absolute of servant leadership.

Let's test this. Your reaction is, "This person is rude." Reorient your mind with a different perspective. Maybe that person had a bad day. Maybe that person had a personal tragedy in his or her life. You don't know and you might never know, but why jump to the worst? Why not give that person the benefit of the doubt?

One person has called me rude several times. What this person fails to see about me is excitement, energy, and quick thinking that sometimes comes off as impulsive or rude. My friends know this about me and give me leeway. My husband whom I love and adore knows this and gives me leeway. But in that moment, this other person can't extend compassion to see me in any other light. And that's okay, compassion isn't a one-way street. In this instance, I have compassion for that person by adjusting how I act. For this one person who called me rude, I go out of my way to be very slow and pointed about what I say. I hold back excitement and a plethora of ideas. And guess what? She doesn't even know it and that's okay.

You can see how you can apply this to so many things you might say to yourself or feel at work. This person offended me. This person didn't include me. This person wrote this email poorly and what huge opportunity email is for misinterpretation. But think about what kind of culture we could be if we exhibited a little compassion and got a little closer to seeing another person's point of view. The best thing is that it costs nothing, except a little vulnerability.

Some of you might argue that last point. Doesn't it cost something if someone else gets the credit? Doesn't it cost something if you are portrayed the wrong way? Doesn't it cost something if you aren't included in an opportunity? Perhaps there is a point there somewhere, but I would argue the baggage you carry from the whole incident and the negative energy involved takes away from what you should be focusing on.

I realized this when I attended a breakout session at the Booth Women conference in Chicago. The session, titled "You're a Threat. Own it," was being presented by a professor, who had taught me Conflict Management when I was a getting my MBA about 15 years ago. I sat in the breakout session with the most incredibly weird feeling as the professor presented this story about a conflict she recently had. Her team was at a client's site where she was trying to get the client to approve funding. One of her colleagues was gasping and huffing in the background as she presented, so much so that the client turned to her colleague and asked if there was an issue. At that point, the colleague told the client that he felt there were gaps in what the professor was presenting.

As I sat there, I could feel the extreme amount of emotion the professor felt at the time. She was embarrassed. She felt betrayed. She was pissed off. All this came through loud and clear in her presentation. But I had a sinking feeling in my gut. The professor went on further to explain how she handled it. She discussed the incident with her colleagues and reviewed her options but felt utterly compelled to do something. That something was writing and sending an email to the huffing and gasping colleague. It read something along the lines of, "Dear colleague, I noticed at our meeting the other day that you had some trouble breathing. In fact, the noise caught the client's attention. Please seek help for this medical condition. In the meantime, please feel free to review the source of my research."

Drop the mic and the professor was proud of herself, but I just felt uncomfortable. Maybe the employee did have a health issue. Or maybe there was something else going on. A death in the family? It was driving me crazy and then I started thinking that as a student in her class, I would have easily sent that email if not more. Fifteen years ago, I might have easily hauled off and said something right in front of the client or more subtly directly thereafter to the colleague. But that wasn't me now and I was empathizing with this colleague I had never met before. And I thought, "Was I now too soft? Too sensitive?"

The professor remarked that she received no reply since that email. A successful professional battle? Had she shushed him up? Put him in his place? What do you think her colleagues thought? Were they listening advocates? Or were they listening and thinking to themselves, "Yeah, it's not worth it," or worst, "She's a bit crazy and I will just agree." I don't know. I just realized at that point that emotion or reacting was not a place I wanted to operate from. There was absolutely no compassion in that decision to send the email. It was protecting the turf. It was pure ego. It was an "I" decision. Who knows what that employee had been going through, but guess what, we all have demons that we are fighting. We all put our pants on the same way, as an employee who worked for me a long time ago often reminded me. What did sending the email really do? Put him on notice not to do it again? I don't think so. I think it just made her feel better. But let's take the client perspective: Perhaps the client felt embarrassed to see the professor's colleague making noises and decided to call him out. Maybe in the client's eyes, the professor didn't lose any credibility.

Another favorite quote from Eleanor Roosevelt is, "No one can make you feel incompetent without your permission." I choose that route. I choose to believe in the value and worth I bring so that I can bridge all the other minor inconveniences life brings me. Sound crazy? Maybe? But I don't think anything would bring me to write that email today. In fact, whenever I find myself reacting with any emotion other than the emotion I use to inspire people, I look to see the other person's perspective. What is possibly in their mind influencing them to act this way? What are they thinking? Then, I see if I can find something, such as in this case perhaps the colleague really does have a medical condition. I look for compassion and let it go.

Why? It's not always easy. There is no way around that. For me, lot of practice and self-reflection and I still need to work at it. It started with the Lean events. I couldn't react in the Lean events because then I wouldn't be helping the team come together and find a solution. You had to check all your feelings and thoughts at the door. No judgement. No frustration. No selfishness. There was no room in the room for "I" or how I felt because I was the glue holding the team together. I was the shepherd ensuring they made it out of the "valley of despair." Every moment in those Lean events matters. But if you are consumed with your vantage point, how you feel and your emotions, you can't possibly be mindful enough to act on those moments.

EVERY MOMENT

Every moment is an opportunity. It might be to help someone with an idea. It might be to engage an employee. It might be to learn something and improve what you're doing. Finding those opportunities starts with the journey to seeing. Seeing what you can change and being willing to look at yourself. Are you finding those opportunities?

It's funny. This part almost didn't make it into the book. I thought I was done. And then I was invited to a workshop where the majority of the team was in person. There were only a few of us on the phone. I had found out just last minute about the meeting and didn't know so many were gathering in person. I would have flown out had I known. It's always odd to have a workshop where most of the team are in the room and only a few on the phone. It started out great though. There was valuable discussion amongst the team, even with those of us on the phone. We had video, which was helpful to see people's faces and the room. The team had some heated debates. And then midstream, rather abruptly, the team in the room gathered at the map on the wall.

It felt weird. The timing of it occurred after some heated discussion, which made it seem like the people in the room just chose to ignore those of us on the phone. I knew that was likely not the case but it was

70

uncomfortable for those of us on the phone. At times, the people on the phone would try to speak up but no one in the room was acknowledging these comments.

Concerned that part of the team (those on the phone) felt left out, I reached out to the leader of the meeting. He implied he gave guidance to someone in the room to cut off the virtual call and just have the team in the room work at the board. He would follow up with those on the phone later. That made sense to me but I explained that I didn't hear any such guidance. I also didn't think the other participants on the phone heard the instructions to drop off. I said some of them were still trying to participate. I say "trying" because no one was listening to them in the room. The video was still going so we could see everything. There was no reason to think the call had ended.

He wrote me back rather insistently that he had given the instructions. Then he went on to tell me how things wrapped up very well. I love to analyze these types of situations. They are little learning lessons and most of what this book is about. Here I was telling this leader, this person who was ultimately in charge of the meeting, that he disengaged two employees. I was offering insight to the team's dynamic. I was offering an opportunity to improve something he had done. An opportunity to improve his influence. And the leader responded with deflection followed by a pat on the back. A pat on his back.

Life is full of these little moments. These opportunities. You just need to be listening and willing to see. It's funny I thought about this inability to just own that action and apologize. What jumped in my head was how I was often angry with myself for apologizing too much. This is often something noted as a weakness in women, so I had become conscious that I did it. Heck, I had been at Panera during lunch. My order got messed up and then I found myself telling the lady how sorry I was as I took the fixed order. I was apologizing for them messing up my order!

As I thought about it more, I realized the process of ordering requires two people. One states the order clearly. The other records it. Simple process but either could be at fault for the order being wrong. It could have been my fault. Maybe I was preoccupied with my kids as I ordered and the lady didn't hear me. It's a team effort when you think about it. There I was saying, "sorry" as I took the fixed order. But the "sorry" wasn't because I thought I did something wrong. I wasn't apologizing for that. The "sorry" was because I sat there and watched the sandwich person hustle. I watched her sweat a little more and her face redden as I just halted the lunch flow at their peak busy time. I saw stress and emotion build in her face. And for that, I was sorry. The "sorry" was because I had empathy for her. Wow, that struck me! "Sorry" was not such a weakness after all. It surfaced because of one of my greatest strengths, compassion.

In the previous example with the employees on the phone, the leader had no empathy. He felt it wasn't his fault. So, it didn't matter how the people on the phone felt. As such, he dismissed their feelings. Heck, he dismissed me, which isn't easy to do. He wasn't on the journey and couldn't see what he could improve. He lost influence in the situation. Influence with those employees on the phone. Influence with me. Every moment is an opportunity. Whether it's an order at Panera or leading a meeting, every moment is an opportunity to do something better. To engage someone. To make a difference.

Think about the things we do so much during our days. Email. Passing someone in the hallway. Is each one of these an opportunity? Yes. Sometimes it's not what you do with the moment. It's what you don't do. Not answering an email is at the top of the list. I can't defend this as I normally do. I can usually find the best in the other person. I can usually find another perspective. But for this one, I don't have it. I have had people talk to me about this. I have experienced it myself. Replying to an email is common courtesy, and the act of not replying can disengage employees. Let me take the story I gave earlier about my mentee. She was desperately searching to find a position. She wanted to stay with Watson Health. I reached out to two leaders I knew. One leader responded to me within a day. She set up time to talk to my mentee and was honest about the positions she had. My mentee was not a fit, but she gave her a name of someone else to contact. This leader also gave her something else. She gave her hope. She took the time to talk to her and at the end of it, reassured her she would make a great contribution to someone's team.

The second leader never replied to me. Such a difference in my personal engagement for these two leaders. I admired the first. I would work for her in a heartbeat but I struggled with the latter. Let me run through my thinking. Maybe he thought he would reach out and forgot to reply. But then why not respond with a simple, "Got it, Laura," which a lot of leaders do. Maybe he thought he couldn't help, but then why not reach out to me and just say, "Hey I appreciate you reaching out, but I don't think I can help." Acceptable. I would have settled for any reply, even a reply that came two months late, saying "I was busy. Here is what I think." But no reply? No reply equals "you don't matter." It means I don't have to reply to you. A whole slew of negative emotions follow the simple act of not replying and there is no counter. It just disengages.

I have made mistakes with email. I always reply but there was an important lesson I recently learned regarding the use of email in general. I was emailing a group where I was following up on some items that needed to be done. Nothing wrong with the email but there was nothing special about it either. The leader of the work stream piggybacked off my email to the group and added the something special. She made it more than a simple follow up of tasks. She reminded the group of the why behind the mechanics. And I thought, "Why didn't I do that?" I was on autopilot and missed that opportunity. I hadn't thought about email in that way before.

Every moment is a chance to communicate or a chance to engage or disengage, whether it's email or passing someone in the hallway. I am intrigued by the people who don't say hi in passing. I can understand it if you're shy or don't know the person. However, there are people I pass in the hallway I have known for years who don't say hi. I always say hi, so that makes it slightly awkward. I think if I was a different person, maybe someone at a higher level, they would say hi. So, like the missing email response, this type of behavior disengages. I do think most of the time, these employees are just on autopilot but from the other person's point of view, it feels like you are not worth the "hi." And like the unanswered email, they lose influence and in some cases, appear unapproachable, which is not what you want as an influential leader.

The last easily missed moment is "thank you." I remember when we ran a thank you campaign. It ran one week and the idea was you would recognize and thank people. Not a bad idea, but I remember thinking, "Why do we need a week or a campaign to thank people?" It should just be part of what you do. Like recording accomplishments or training monthly, writing a thank you should be a monthly task you review and complete. But again, not on autopilot. It is an opportunity to engage. Personalize it. Add something special. At some point I started writing the teams from Lean events a very personalized thank-you. Why? Because it was an opportunity to inspire. It was an opportunity to help them carry the energy from being in the room together forward as they continuously worked on process changes after the event. Sometimes the thank-you's started with something funny. Sometimes they gave the team something to think about, but they were always specialized and based on something the team experienced that week. Here is a specialized thank-you I sent to a team from a Lean event:

Thank you all again for an AWESOME week! My daughter and I went to Panera after I picked her up. As I was standing there waiting for the food, I noticed the Panera had a huddle board reading "Gold standard: let's be the example!" At first, I was cracking up at the Gold Standard and thinking, geez this event is following me around. But then I looked a little further and I love the line, "let's be the example!"

I mentioned when we kicked off on Monday that in our work we study change and transformation. Historically, transformation is sustained when people unite in favor of something. I mentioned winning in 2018 as an example, but given this week, your group has another compelling reason. Unite around this team and the hard work you did this week!

Be the example and carry BOLD change forward! Thank you so much again for all your hard work this week, and what is to come in the next month as you sustain this process.

Please feel free to ping me with any questions! Laura

At the heart of this event was a review the team called "Gold Team." It had been at the center for most of the week's discussion. Different people had different views over what words meant. Reviews were named by colors. After spending a significant amount of time discussing what "Gold Team" meant to everyone, the team decided to change the name. Sometimes it's easier to start new rather than correct bad habits that are engrained in the workforce. I just happened to notice the sign at Panera and the tie to the gold color. I loved the tag line, "let's be the example!" Then I used all this to make the thank-you something special. Personalized and inspiring.

Why do all this, right? I know. It takes extra time. It is extra work. True, but I think I referenced earlier that I like to refer to quotes. "Unless someone like you cares a whole awful lot, nothing is going to get better. It's not," says the Lorax from children's stories. That's how I felt. I wasn't doing all this for some gain. I was back at my childhood roots and doing it because if felt right.

This journey to seeing changed me personally as a leader, wife, mother, colleague, and friend. I carry it with me everywhere I go. It's not something I turn on and off, although it is something I still need to work at. Just like every moment is a chance to engage employees, it is also a chance to help a neighbor or a friend. To make a connection with someone you can learn from or to send a little good out into the world to someone who needs it.

It's easier than you think. These opportunities are just sitting there right in front of all of us. We just need to be willing to see and act on them. I was out with one of the team members and after dinner, we decided to stop at a local CVS Pharmacy. We picked up water and snacks, which were cheaper at CVS than the hotel. I was in the middle of checking out and I noticed something that really bothered me. So, after we were both done, I pulled the colleague aside and I said, "Quick Lean lesson. At the heart of Lean is respect for people. What do you see at CVS about that checkout line?" She was smart and pointed out all kinds of waste and then ideas. Move this or that. Great ideas really, but that wasn't at the core of what was bothering me. I asked to take a closer look and she still didn't see it. So, I told her. The lady checking us out was elderly. I applaud CVS for employing her but she was standing at the checkout counter with her oxygen tank and walker right in front her. Standing. I told my colleague that I would be writing CVS that night and telling them they need to get her a chair. There was no reason she had to be standing. They could even adjust the whole area so that you could barely tell she was sitting, if they did it right. It was just simple stuff.

I couldn't turn it off. Most of us in the Lean world went into this position because we love to fix things and improve the work employees do. When I encounter problems, I often go into coach mode. Sometimes I think I can fix just about anything. My husband and I were at Universal Studios with the kids. Our oldest was not feeling well so we let her stay back in the hotel room and chill. We took our son with us to the lobby area and sat for a drink. We were having an enjoyable conversation when the couple's conversation next to us started escalating. It was one of those attempts. Go to a public space and have a normal conversation but when it's a matter of the heart, that is never a great idea.

I often default to facilitator mode. I was thinking as I listened, "He's making a valid point but might need to listen more." She had to dial back the emotion. Overreacting. I was so close to saying something. I wanted to say, "Life is hard enough. Why make it harder?" I wanted to say, "Compassion. Compassion. Compassion. Especially for those closest to us." But my husband motioned me a look of "don't" and I stayed put. And my son soon tired, so we decided I would take him back while my husband finished his beer.

When my husband returned, he remarked, "Poor Larry."

"Poor Larry?" I get it. The husband was Larry. My husband continued to tell me how the whole conversation escalated to the point where his wife finally screamed, "Larry, you just don't get it!" My husband was joking. Perhaps a bad joke, but it was sad. There was no winner in that situation. They both lose. I still wonder about that couple and whether I should have said something. Something that would have made them think. Something that would have softened the situation so they could hear each other, just as I often did in Lean events.

The good news is in most other situations you can say something. You can make a joke or strike up a conversation. I always find it funny how something can be a simple inconvenience and people act like it is the most serious situation. A great example is to watch a long line at the grocery store. Responses such as huffing and puffing and stares from people as they wait in line. An inconvenience, I agree, but again letting that frustration build and mount only means you miss something else. In this case for me, a perfectly nice conversation I had with someone next to me as we waited.

It doesn't cost you anything but can make such a difference for the other person. The after-school care program at my children's school was putting in a new payment system. There were a few things they were struggling with but for putting in a new system, the invoices were much clearer than before. The communication was good. So, I simply thanked the admin and told her a few compliments. She replied surprised and said that of all the parents who had reached out, I was the first to say something positive. I told her I was familiar with how hard installations like these could be and I don't think everyone knew that. A few kind words made all the difference to that person who was working so hard.

A CALL TO ACTION

What carries me through the hard times is believing. Just like the old Journey song, which sometimes does play in my head, "Don't stop believing." Believing in what? It's believing in the best of what life has to offer. It's believing in your purpose and what you can give. In Lean we often say, "Act your way into a new way of thinking." But I don't think its half bad to control your thinking as well. Redirecting your mind to the positive or the ideal scenario is powerful. For me, what better use of my tenacity than believing? That's a heck of a thing to be stubborn about. I believe in this book. I believe this book is going to reach people and give them something to consider. I envision a scenario where I get to speak and share this journey with Watson Health. And it's not because I am full of myself; it's because that is the gift I have to give. Speaking. Inspiring. It's not about making money or getting my name out there. I believe in sharing my journey, others will start or continue their journey with new insights. I know some of you are thinking, "What Kool-aid is this gal drinking?" If I let myself get bogged down with this, I would never get anywhere. You can study this in people like Jim Carrey, the actor. Oprah interviewed Jim Carrey about his start. Before becoming a famous actor, Jim Carrey was poor and trying to make it. Jim would visualize (believe) that he was going to achieve fame and fortune. He wrote a check to himself for $10 million for "acting services rendered" dating it November 1995. He carried the check in his wallet and he continuously looked for work as an actor. Just before the expiration, Jim landed the part Dumb and Dumber for $10 million. Now, it's not just the belief. Jim had to work hard and hustle. But the combination has to be there.

Stories are important for believing and transformation. Many times, the teams will reference the story for learning during the week. Other times it becomes something the team can bond over—a rule or joke. At the heart of it, there's a lesson to learn or something to be inspired by. So, I leave you with one last story that I carry with me in inspiring bold at Watson Health.

There was an elderly man who had been found, passed out in the stairway of his house. His wife was gardening and found him unconscious. She called the ambulance and he was rushed urgently to the hospital. Later that day, their daughter traveled in to help and support her mother. It was hard. Her father was unconscious. He had several similar attacks like these since she was young. It felt familiar. It felt like he would snap out of it. He had done this so many times before. The neurologist came by and recounted the time her father had been without oxygen. Thirty some minutes between her mother calling the ambulance, the time at the house and the time at the hospital. The chance of brain activity was slim upon resuscitation.

Unfortunately, the man had been in the hospital before. The man had asked his wife to give him time if he went under again. He always made it out. "Don't pull the plug right away, Margie," he told his wife jokingly. But now that exact situation the man envisioned lay before his wife and daughter. The wife could not bring herself to make the decision to remove him from life support, and in her mind put to death the man she had loved for a lifetime. The daughter was clueless. She had no medical background and knew the situation seemed inhumane but how do you at that moment influence someone to let their partner of a lifetime go. The night came and his vitals fell. The doctor from the ER rushed in. Mom and daughter were escorted outside while the medical team injected medicine and revived the man. This ritual carried on a few times during the night.

It escalated when the ER doctor stormed up to revitalize the man once again. But this time, the ER doctor was going to force the DNR. She emphatically told the wife, "I don't have time to keep coming up here and reviving him. Sign the DNR." Where was compassion? Where was any thought over the client in this situation? Such a cold ruthless ending for a couple who had known each other since they were 16. Wrong or right, the daughter went in fighting. "My mom is not ready," the daughter exclaimed, "So until she is, you will bring your butt up here and do your job!" The mother was comforted, although the daughter wasn't.

Soon after, the man expired. The mother still to this day asks the daughter, "Did I sign the DNR? I didn't, right?"

"No mother, you didn't. It was just his time to go," explained the daughter.

At the heart of my purpose, this is the story I carry with me. At Watson Health, we talk about physician burnout. In this case, the processes that consumed and overburdened the ER doctor so much that she had so little compassion at a critical time of need for that family. The neurologist who was ill-equipped to convince the wife onto a more humane path for her husband. The hospital that delivered the most miserable experience ever.

At Watson Health, we talk about helping the person at the end of the process and in this story, the mother and daughter. I carry this story with me as fuel for my purpose because in this story, the daughter is me. The wife and husband are my mother and father. I know as I help make employees' work easier and coach to build better leaders, I am doing my part to help the people at the end of the process.

There is a certain peace that comes along with this realization that has reinvigorated me. I point my children to follow what they love to do. That's where you get your energy and that's where you find your value. I challenge you to find your story and your calling and carry that with you as you continue your journey and take these insights to change the world. Thank you for allowing me to share my journey to inspire bold and change in the world.

ABOUT THE AUTHOR

Laura Kempf is a Business Transformation Consultant at IBM Watson Health. Since the beginning of the company's Lean journey, she has been influencing the Lean transformation by leading teams in monthly lean events using breakthrough thinking to improve processes.

In 2006, Kempf joined the IBM Watson Health Finance department and held several positions, including overseeing the accounting functions as sole Accounting Manager after being acquired by a private equity firm. As Director of Government Finance, she led teams to transform their current order to cash system to a government accounting system, a feat government auditors remarked later as impossible.

Kempf received a Bachelor of Science in Chemical Engineering from Purdue University and an MBA from the University of Chicago. She is adjunct professor at Oakland University (Lean Leadership) and actively participates in Michigan Lean Consortium. As Detroit City Ambassador for Booth Women, Kempf promotes staying connected and networking with University of Chicago (Booth business school).

Kempf is thrilled she has reconnected with her love of writing. At 10 years old, she began to write and submit her work to publishers. She loves and appreciates her husband, Scott, and two children, Elise and Lincoln, who have always supported all her endeavors.

Reference Kempf's blog site at www.inspiringbold.com and follow her on Twitter (@inspiringbold) and LinkedIn.